W9-BVL-382

STAR SIGNS

Virginia Loh-Hagan

45TH PARALLEL PRESS

Published in the United States of America by Cherry Lake Publishing Group
Ann Arbor, Michigan
www.cherrylakepublishing.com

Reading Adviser: Marla Conn, MS, Ed., Literacy specialist, Read-Ability, Inc.
Book Designer: Felicia Macheske

Photo Credits: © Daxiao Productions/Shutterstock.com, cover; © TerraceStudio/Shutterstock.com, cover; © Zolotarevs/Shutterstock.com, 5; © maradon 333/Shutterstock.com, 6; © Zhuravlev Andrey/Shutterstock.com, 9; © Alberto_Gonzalez_Gimenez/Shutterstock.com, 11; © Dimitrios/Shutterstock.com, 12; © Gelpi/Shutterstock.com, 15; © Pixel-Shot/Shutterstock.com, 17; Ricardo Reitmeyer/Shutterstock.com, 18; © TeamDAF/Shutterstock.com, 20; © Lisa F. Young/Shutterstock.com, 22; © Photosani/Shutterstock.com, 25; © pjcross/Shutterstock.com, 27; © Kamira/Shutterstock.com, 29; © LeoShoot/Shutterstock.com, 30

Graphics Throughout: © AKaiser/Shutterstock.com; © galastudio/Shutterstock.com; © tanyabosyk/Shutterstock.com; © ViSnezh/Shutterstock.com; © MARINA ARABADZHI/Shutterstock.com; © Alisa Burkovska/Shutterstock.com

45th Parallel Press is an imprint of Cherry Lake Publishing Group.

Library of Congress Cataloging-in-Publication Data

Names: Loh-Hagan, Virginia, author.
Title: Star signs / by Virginia Loh-Hagan.
Description: Ann Arbor, Michigan : Cherry Lake Publishing, 2020. | Series: Who are you? | Includes index.
Identifiers: LCCN 2020007002 (print) | LCCN 2020007003 (ebook) | ISBN 9781534169173 (hardcover) | ISBN 9781534170858 (paperback) | ISBN 9781534172692 (pdf) | ISBN 9781534174535 (ebook)
Subjects: LCSH: Zodiac—Juvenile literature. | Astrology—Juvenile literature.
Classification: LCC BF1726 .L64 2020 (print) | LCC BF1726 (ebook) | DDC 133.5/2—dc23
LC record available at https://lccn.loc.gov/2020007002
LC ebook record available at https://lccn.loc.gov/2020007003

Cherry Lake Publishing Group would like to acknowledge the work of the Partnership for 21st Century Learning, a Network of Battelle for Kids. Please visit http://www.battelleforkids.org/networks/p21 for more information.

Printed in the United States of America
Corporate Graphics

Dr. Virginia Loh-Hagan is an author, university professor, and former classroom teacher. She was born on June 14. She's a Gemini. She lives in San Diego, California, with her very tall husband and very naughty dogs. To learn more about her, visit www.virginialoh.com.

Chapter One

SUN OR STARS?

What is a zodiac sign? What is astrology? How are star signs and elements connected?

"What's your sign?" Today, this is a common greeting. A person's sign is based on the position of the sun at one's birth. The position is placed within one of the **zodiac** signs. The zodiac is an area of the sky. The sun, moon, stars, and planets move in this area. The zodiac is divided into 12 parts. Each part has a collection of stars. Each collection is called a **constellation**. These constellations form a shape. The shapes are connected with a time of year. Each shape has a name and a **symbol**. Symbols are things or signs. They stand for an idea. These symbols are called sun signs or, more commonly, star signs.

Take the quiz at the end of this book. What is your sign?

Some people believe these symbols affect humans. These symbols control people's personalities. They control people's relationships. They control people's **destinies**. Destinies are people's futures.

Star sign **astrology** is also called Western astrology. **Astronomy** is a science. It's the study of outer space. Astrology is a practice. It looks at how space objects affect human lives. Astrologers study the positions of the sun, stars, and planets. They study the angles. They believe all things are connected. They make **horoscopes**. Horoscopes are special circle charts. They map the sun, stars, and planets. They map these things at a specific time. Astrologers use these charts. They **divine** information about people's lives. Divine means to interpret.

Each zodiac sign has a house. Learn more about these houses. What is your star sign's house?

FUN FACTS

* Ancient Egyptians looked for the rising of Sirius. Ancient means a long time ago. Sirius is called the Dog Star. It's the brightest star in the night sky. This star rises in Egypt around mid-July. Ancient Egyptians saw Sirius as a sign of the Nile's yearly flooding.

* Elsbeth Ebertin lived from 1880 to 1944. She was a German astrologer. She predicted Adolf Hitler's rise to power. She was also the astrologer for the king of Bulgaria.

* Benjamin Franklin lived from 1706 to 1790. He was one of the Founding Fathers of the United States. He was also a prankster. He had a friend named Titan Leeds. Franklin used astrology. He predicted Leeds's death in his almanac. Almanacs are books with dates. He did this as a joke. Leeds didn't die. Franklin said he was a ghost.

* Ophiuchus is a big constellation. It's shaped like a man holding a snake. It's called the "13th sign of the zodiac." There are only 12 months. So, Ophiuchus was dropped as a star sign.

Star sign astrology has 12 signs. Each sign stands for a period of a year. Each sign has different personalities. The 12 signs are also divided into 4 elements. The elements are fire, air, earth, and water.

Fire and air are **masculine** signs. Masculine means manly. Fire signs are Aries, Leo, and Sagittarius. They're full of passion. Air signs are Libra, Aquarius, and Gemini. They're smart. They're curious.

Water and earth are **feminine** signs. Feminine means womanly. Water signs are Cancer, Scorpio, and Pisces. They have a lot of feelings. Earth signs are Capricorn, Taurus, and Virgo. They get things done.

Each zodiac sign has ruling planets. These planets help define a person's energy. What are your star sign's ruling planets?

9

Chapter Two

STARS OVER TIME

Why did ancient cultures look at the stars? Who is William Lilly? Who is R. H. Naylor?

Ancient Chinese people looked at the stars. They charted time. They also used stars to divine **omens**. Omens are signs. They predict good or bad times.

Ancient Babylonians also looked at the stars. They predicted seasons. Today, ancient Babylonia is Iraq. They predicted natural disasters. They tracked the gods. They wanted to divine the gods' wishes. They made the oldest known horoscope. This horoscope is dated April 29, 410 BCE. It describes the night sky. It's on a stone tablet.

Ptolemy was an ancient Greek. He identified the constellations. He wrote about the 12 star signs. He started the year when the sun appeared in Aries. Aries is a constellation. This is the first day of spring.

People used stars to make calendars. Knowing the seasons helped farmers. They kept track of when to plant. How are calendars useful to you?

Ancient Romans learned from the ancient Greeks. They also believed in star signs. The names of star signs came from the ancient Romans. Astrology spread around the world. People used it for advice.

William Lilly lived from 1602 to 1681 CE. He lived in England. He wrote books about astrology. He made predictions. He wrote them in an almanac. They have information about these dates. Lilly did this every year. His almanacs were very popular. He made a lot of money. Some people believed him. Some people didn't. He was called the "English Merlin." Merlin is a famous wizard character.

Many words came from the ancient Greeks and Romans.
Can you think of some of these words?

EXPLAINED BY
SCIENCE

Bertram Forer lived from 1914 to 2000. He was a psychologist. He gave personality tests to students. All the students got the same content. But the students thought the content was unique to them. The Forer effect happens when people trust personality descriptions. These descriptions are vague. But people think they're specific to them. They shape the descriptions to fit themselves. Some scientists say the Forer effect is why people believe in astrology. People who read horoscopes make their horoscopes work for them. People want to have hope. They can take the bad things if they know good things are happening. The Forer effect is also called the Barnum effect. It's named after P. T. Barnum. Barnum was a showman. He was famous for his circus. He said his shows "had something for everyone."

R. H. Naylor lived from 1889 to 1952. He was English. He was the first star sign astrologer. He wrote the first newspaper horoscopes. He wrote predictions and advice for each star sign. He became famous on August 24, 1930. Princess Margaret was born only a few days later. The *Sunday Express* newspaper asked Naylor to write her star chart. Naylor predicted her life would be "eventful." He predicted big things would happen in her seventh year. He made more predictions. His predictions came true. Readers loved his reports. This inspired other newspapers to include horoscopes.

Scientists doubted astrology. They said it wasn't a science. Astrology became more of an art.

Read your horoscope. What does it say? Do you think it's true?

Chapter Three

STAR POWERS

What are the 12 star signs? What are the personality traits of each star sign?

Aries is a ram. These types blaze trails. They like to start new things. They take risks. They compete. They like to win. They have a lot of energy. They're good inventors. They're funny. They're honest. But they can be impatient. They can be self-centered.

Taurus is a bull. These types are cautious. They move carefully. They use common sense. They can be counted on. They love being in nature. They like to relax. They like to enjoy life. But they can be stubborn. They don't like change.

Gemini is the twins. These types have 2 sides. They like to do several things at once. They're smart. They do things quickly. They talk a lot. They have open minds. They're creative. But they tend to exaggerate. They can juggle too much.

Some people hire astrologers. Would you hire one?
Why or why not?

Cancer is a crab. These types fit in anywhere. Their gut feelings are strong. They're sensitive. They're quick to defend themselves. They protect their loved ones. They feel for others. But their moods can change quickly. They might hold on to grudges.

Leo is a lion. These types are full of life. They're playful. They like being the center of attention. They get people to like them. They're leaders. But they can be bossy. They can be prideful.

Virgo is a **maiden**. Maidens are young girls. These types are modest. They're logical. They're organized. They're tidy. They like things to be perfect. They work hard to improve themselves. They practice a lot. They solve problems. But they can be too critical. They can be anxious.

Read more about these star signs.
What are their strengths? What are their weaknesses?

Libra is **scales** of justice. Scales are tools. They're used to weigh things. These types want balance. They want peace. They want harmony. But they may have a hard time making decisions. They don't like conflict.

Scorpio is a scorpion. These types are powerful. They like to be in charge. They're passionate. They're driven. They're not afraid to change. But they tend to not forgive easily. They can be jealous.

Sagittarius is an **archer**. Archers shoot bows and arrows. These types like adventures. They're positive. They see opportunities. They want success. But they can be lazy. They can be irresponsible.

Libra is the only star sign whose symbol is a thing.
Why do you think this is?

CONNECTION

The Capricorn goat is actually a hybrid. Hybrids are a combination of 2 animals. The Capricorn goat is a sea-goat. It has a goat's head and body. It has a fish's tail. In real life, there is a goat hybrid. It's called a geep. It's a cross between a goat and a sheep. This is rare. Goats and sheep may look alike. But they don't usually mate. They belong to different animal groups. Babies of goats and sheep rarely live. In 1988, a live geep was born in France. In 1990, a live geep was born in New Zealand. In 2000, a live geep was born in Africa. In 2013, a live geep was born in Ireland. In 2014, a live geep was born in Scottsdale, Arizona. It was born in a petting zoo. It's named Butterfly. Butterfly's mom was a sheep. Her dad was a goat. Butterfly has a goat face and feet. She's covered in wool.

Capricorn is a goat. These types are planners. They take time to meet their goals. They play things safe. They like to be alone. They're private. They're humble. But they can be stubborn. They don't like to be wrong.

Aquarius is a person who carries water. These types are special. They're odd in a good way. They do their own thing. They're unpredictable. They like exploring. But they can be **rebels**. Rebels are people who break the rules.

Pisces is a fish. These types like all things magical. They have great imaginations. They have big dreams. They can keep secrets. They're gentle. They're selfless. They reflect on their feelings. They go with the flow. But they can be unrealistic. They might lack boundaries.

Aquarius is the most humanitarian star sign. This means they want to improve people's lives. They serve the community. Do you know any Aquarius types?

Chapter Four

FAMOUS EXAMPLES

Who is J. P. Morgan? Who is Mae West? Who is Queen Elizabeth I?

Cardinal signs are Aries, Cancer, Libra, and Capricorn. Cardinal means important. These star signs are the start of new seasons. These personality types take action. They start projects. They take charge before others do. They react. They respond.

J. P. Morgan was born on April 17, 1837. This means he's an Aries. Morgan founded many banks. He had railroads. He had companies. He changed American business. He was very rich. He was very powerful. He had astrologers. These astrologers helped him make business deals. Morgan may have said, "Millionaires don't use astrology. Billionaires do."

Figure out the signs of your family members.
Do they act like their star signs?

Fixed signs are Taurus, Leo, Scorpio, and Aquarius. Fixed means not changing. These star signs happen in the middle of seasons. These personality types are steady. They keep moving. They don't quit.

Mae West was born on August 17, 1893. This means she's a Leo. West was a movie star. She was a singer. She was a writer. She started performing at age 7. She kept working for 80 years. Some people didn't like her work. They tried to get her to quit. But nothing stopped her. It's believed she used star charts. She got advice from an astrologer.

People get help in different ways.
When you need advice, what do you do?

BIOGRAPHY

Ophira and Tali Edut are identical twin sisters. They went to the University of Michigan. At age 19, they had their star charts read. This was a birthday present. They said, "It was eerie, actually, how well it described us . . . We became obsessed and started doing all of our friends' charts and even guessing random people's signs at parties." They're now professional astrologers. They call themselves AstroTwins. They have a website. They're the official astrologers for *Elle* magazine. They write for other media sources as well. They write books about astrology. They've been on several TV and radio shows. They've been interviewed for several magazines. They read star charts of famous people. Their clients include Emma Roberts and Beyoncé. They live in New York City, New York, and Seattle, Washington. They said, "Now we know that astrology is the ultimate tool and shortcut to understanding what makes people tick. We think of it as the blueprint to your soul."

Mutable signs are Gemini, Virgo, Sagittarius, and Pisces. Mutable means likely to change. These star signs happen at the end of the seasons. They change into new seasons. These personality types change as needed. They're flexible. They make peace. They can take on different roles.

Queen Elizabeth I was born on September 7, 1533. This means she's a Virgo. She was queen of England and Ireland. Her rule was called the Golden Age. She was one of the most powerful rulers ever. She defeated the Spanish Armada. She brought peace. She expanded England. She had her own astrologer named John Dee. Dee advised her on many things. He came up with the term "British Empire."

Many leaders have advisers. Who are your advisers?

29

WHO ARE YOU?
TAKE THE QUIZ!

When were you born? Your birthdate determines your star sign.

- **March 21–April 19:** Aries
- **April 20–May 20:** Taurus
- **May 21–June 20:** Gemini
- **June 21–July 22:** Cancer
- **July 23–August 22:** Leo
- **August 23–September 22:** Virgo
- **September 23–October 22:** Libra

- **October 23–November 21:** Scorpio
- **November 22–December 21:** Sagittarius
- **December 22–January 19:** Capricorn
- **January 20–February 18:** Aquarius
- **February 19–March 20:** Pisces

What is your lucky number? Some people believe numbers have special powers.

- **Aries:** 5
- **Taurus:** 6
- **Gemini:** 7
- **Cancer:** 2
- **Leo:** 19
- **Virgo:** 7

- **Libra:** 3
- **Scorpio:** 4
- **Sagittarius:** 6
- **Capricorn:** 4
- **Aquarius:** 22
- **Pisces:** 11

What is your birth stone? Some people believe birth stone will give its owner extra luck.

- **Aries:** Bloodstone
- **Taurus:** Sapphire
- **Gemini:** Agate
- **Cancer:** Emerald
- **Leo:** Onyx
- **Virgo:** Carnelian
- **Libra:** Chrysolite
- **Scorpio:** Beryl
- **Sagittarius:** Citrine
- **Capricorn:** Ruby
- **Aquarius:** Garnet
- **Pisces:** Amethyst

What color should you use to decorate your house? Some colors will help you relax better.

- **Aries:** Sand
- **Taurus:** Teakwood
- **Gemini:** Onyx
- **Cancer:** Silver
- **Leo:** Jungle Green
- **Virgo:** Buttercream Yellow
- **Libra:** Chocolate Brown
- **Scorpio:** Midnight Blue
- **Sagittarius:** Pale Peach
- **Capricorn:** Mushroom
- **Aquarius:** Gunmetal Gray
- **Pisces:** Lavender

GLOSSARY

archer (AHRCH-ur) person who shoots bow and arrows

astrology (uh-STRAH-luh-jee) the practice of how space objects like stars affect the lives of humans

astronomy (uh-STRAH-nuh-mee) the study or science of outer space

cardinal (KAHR-duh-nuhl) important

constellation (kahn-stuh-LAY-shuhn) collection of stars that form a shape

destinies (DES-tuh-neez) fates or futures

divine (dih-VINE) to discover or interpret

feminine (FEM-uh-nin) womanly

fixed (FIKSD) permanent

horoscopes (HOR-uh-skopes) special circle charts that map the positions and angles of the sun, stars, and planets

maiden (MAY-duhn) a young woman who is not married

masculine (MAS-kyuh-lin) manly

mutable (MYOO-tuh-buhl) changing, flexible

omens (OH-muhnz) signs that predict good or bad times

rebels (REB-uhlz) people who break the rules

scales (SKAYLZ) tools used to weigh things

symbol (SIM-buhl) thing or sign that stands for an idea

zodiac (ZOH-dee-ak) an imaginary band in the heavens centered on the paths of all the space objects and divided into 12 constellations or signs for astrological purposes

INDEX